Granny
& Papa

A Living Portrait

Stories of the St̓át̓imcets Speaking People

Happy Reading
Malihathur

To my sons

Clayton E J Therrien

Jarrod Denis Therrien

and

in loving memory of

Lillian (Peters) Hillman

Alexis Eric Hillman

All rights reserved.
No part of this publication may be
reproduced or transmitted in any form or
by any means without the
prior written permission of the publisher.

First self published in Canada 2013
ISBN 978-1-304-10403-8
ww.lulu.com ID: 13878502

Copyright © 2013 Malihatkwa Gwen Therrien
Cover illustrations copyright © by Lorenz, Sto:lo Nation, age 9, 2011

Graphic and book design by Mady Graphic Design, Mission BC, Canada

Granny & Papa

A Living Portrait

Stories of the Sťáťimcets Speaking People

by Malihatkwa Gwen Therrien

self published

Acknowledgements

My maternal grandfather, Kukwpi (Chief)

Nkasusa Harry Peters, spiritual mentor

Emma & jacob who inspired me; asking for stories about their ancestors

Kukwpi, Chief Darrell Bob, chief and spiritual leader

Stanley Peters Sr. R.I.P., who said:
"It's good someone remembers the way we used to do things"

Herman Dan & Ken McDonald, Ucwalmi'cwts language words.

All My Relations

Prologue

This is a story of the Transition time. A time when two cultures clashed together, changing both in ways yet to be understood. A time when 'gold fever' brought hordes of men, with only one goal: to get as much of the metal as they could by any means they could. The gold miners and those who profited from these events came and went within a few short years, but the after effects and repercussions are with us today. This is a story of the resilience of the Human Spirit of the Ucwalmicw of the Southern Státimcets Nation to survive and grow strong once again, while adapting to circumstances beyond our control. These stories relate to our 'Rites Of Passage' as we practiced them before and after contact with foreign nations.

Malihatkwa Gwen Therrien

1   *Granny & Papa*

It was an exciting day for the host community of today's events. Family groups had been arriving for the past week. The first two days were occupied with the business of the surrounding Territory Leaders. There were no infringements or threats from the borders of the territory. Disputes were heard and settled after full discussion and agreements arrived at. The Sto:lo came in their canoes on Harrison Lake. The Sto:lo were bringing a bride from their Territory at Sts'ailis to marry a young leader among the Xa'xtsa people. This alliance had been agreed upon when the children were very young. It was the custom, alliance through marriage created strong kinship bonds. The Sto:lo people were very impressive, travelling in huge cedar canoes. The lead canoe carried the warriors and chiefs. The middle canoes carried the women and children, next came the cargo canoe, with supplies for the gathering and trade items. The last canoe was manned by warriors, their responsibility being the safety of the travellers. The marriage alliance ceremony would take place on the last day of the gathering. The families of the young couple knew each other and met at other gatherings over the years. This alliance would bring prestige and honour to both villages of the couple. The young woman came from Sts'ailis and the young man was from the host community, Xa'xtsa. The marriage/alliance had been planned by both families and was the highlight of this year's gathering. The Sto:lo had a place reserved for their canoes and their cargo. The women stood around trying to catch a glimpse of the items to be distributed. An elder cast a frown at them and they scattered like guilty children.

This was an occasion where the people wore their finest traditional outfits. This was a meeting of nation to nation. Woven inner cedar bark garments of the finest quality, lined with feathers of birds for softness, skirts and capes; the women wore their inner cedar bark woven hats to keep the sun out of their eyes. The leaders wore Eagle headdresses with other feathers as a mark of distinction. The Sto:lo Chief wore a woven woollen blanket over his left shoulder and his people all wore cedar hats as well.

The people on the shore were similarly dressed and stood on the shore drumming and singing a welcoming song for their relatives. After ceremonial welcomes were completed, everyone changed into other clothing. After the celebration a few relatives would remain in the village throughout the winter months until spring break up when travel was possible once again. Other groups had arrived by buckboard wagon with a team of horses with provisions for the host community. Others came from north, through the high mountains, while other families' relatives came across the mountains through the Stega'yn (Stein Valley). Every new arrival was greeted warmly and made comfortable and a place found for them to sleep, and food was hot and ready for them as well.

This year's Gathering would take place at Xa'xtsa, located at the head of Harrison Lake. Xa'xtsa is at the Southern edge of the Státimcets speaking people. Today's activities were being hosted by Samahquam. The newest member of the community would be receiving her name. She is the first great grandchild; Granny and Papa's grand daughter had an arranged marriage with a young leader from Lil'wat, which had taken place two summers before at the annual gathering.

Her cousin would be having a ceremony today as well. The proud great grandparents, who are the hosts today, stepped out together while the final preparations were being completed.

Granny felt Papa's hand slip out of hers. Granny realized that he was remembering other times before now, when he was a child visiting this village with his parents. The village sat on the ruins of the old village which had existed on the landscape for hundreds of years.

Papa's grandparents had lived in the Longhouse on the beach by the lake. The longhouse was 300 feet long, small in comparison to the longhouses in the neighbouring territory of the Sto:lo. Papa drew in a deep breath remembering the smell of the cedar plank walls and roof. He thought of the troughs that captured the rain water. He drew in another deep breath, feeling and sensing the warm smell of the earth on the tiered sleeping platform. Reeds and boughs were set down and the familiar sense of peacefulness came over him once again. He felt the blankets made of dog hair and silky goat hair, mixed with stinging nettle fibers, and wild hemp covering him with warmth.

Papa's thoughts flitted over cherished memories, moving into the Longhouse at the end of summer. He felt the warmth of the longhouse, which was heated with radiant heat by a special process. It involved removing soil to a depth of ten inches and replacing it with sand, which was then covered with fine blue clay, fire pits strategically placed throughout the house, to keep the longhouse warm. It still brought a smile of remembrance to his face.

Granny took a few moments to reminisce that she and Papa were children when the 'hairy people' first entered the Territory. These strangers were the gold miners. They had hairy faces, they were dirty and hungry and smelly too. Granny remembered the strange animals they brought with them, not just the donkeys, cattle and horses, but the camels. These animals scared everything. Not only were these camels strange looking, but they had a strong odour. They were stubborn animals and spit a gooey gob when angered.

In Granny and Papa's lifetime, strangers had come into the Territory seeking and taking gold and timber and constructing houses of a different fashion, like boxes with stairs indoors and floors where people slept. The peaked roofs made the snow slide off the roof, just as snow had fallen from the longhouse roof. Papa remembered the' hairy people' had torn apart the village and moved the local people across the way. They had replaced the long house and istken with their style of houses. The gold miners had used the resources of the land without regard. Then, in their hurry, they abandoned the village they had built. Thus began the many changes that would affect the people' way of life. The people moved into these abandoned houses giving up the old way of living communally.

Granny gave Papa's hand a squeeze to bring his attention back to the present time. They gazed around the village, secure in the knowledge that they were unmolested by foreign influences and misunderstandings of their traditions and culture. The Sama7 had left the village and would be away for a few weeks, gathering provisions for the coming winter months.

Gifts were ready for baby. Other gifts awaited the 'give-away', following the feast. The give-away would be given by granddaughter Blue Thunderbird Sky Dancer, who had received her name in her coming of age ceremony earlier in the year.

Every cook made her 'specialty', cakes, and pies, the aromas tickled the nose with every breath. The savoury smells of roasting meat and vegetables competed with each other. Fresh picked greens were in the coolers. Last harvest season's berries and other jarred fruit were mixed together with fresh fruit to create a collage of colour.

The men of the village had caught the salmon a few weeks ago and the salmon had been 'wind dried'. Fish prepared in this manner will keep for a long time. It is a winter staple and in high demand in the bartering and trading system that still exists today. Elk and moose meat were roasting in ovens and grills outside.

Fresh caught salmon was cooking in the traditional way, called 't'a'qsa7'. The salmon was split down along the back bone and cleaned, then skewered with properly cut cedar sticks, crosswise. Uncle Joe was good at preparing the sticks for the barbeque salmon. Other cedar was cut into three foot lengths by one inch round, then split again, almost to the top, in this manner, the salmon could be inserted lengthwise and tied down to hold the salmon securely in place. The end of the three foot sticks was sharpened so that they could be pushed firmly into the ground around the open fire barbeque pit. The salmon was then evenly arranged around the fire pit to allow the fish to cook properly.

The firemen had prepared the fire pit and had the fire ready with plenty of hot coals. The fire had to be maintained at a steady heat. The men shared camaraderie as they worked and visited and got caught up with each other's news. The men took turns turning the salmon so that it cooked thoroughly and evenly. The salmon splattered fat onto the firewood, creating more delicious smells.

The 'Fire Keepers' always arrived at the feast site early, usually a day or so ahead of the gathering. The first fire was the 'Sacred Fire', which burned 24 hours a day during the gathering and allowed to burn itself out as the people travelled home, always under the watchful eyes of the head Fire Keeper.

Children learned early in life not to throw anything into the sacred fire. Every child wished to avoid an elders' frown or 'the look'. Lessons were taught to children by way of a story telling, sometimes at bedtime a scary story might be told about the naughty boy or girl who misbehaved during a gathering.

Granny and Papa were satisfied that everything was ready for the festivities to begin. There was a hum of anticipation in the air as everyone gathered together. "Old Griz," made his entrance. Papa raised his hand, the assembled company hushed. Papa made his presentation of a woven blanket, with tobacco from the territory, with a red woven bandana on top.

The Medicine Man was simply known as Old Griz and was accepted as such. Old Griz wore his sash of office over his right shoulder and covering his heart and pinned it over his left hip and he wore the red woven bandana around his head. He had prepared himself spiritually. He painted his face with red ochre. Old Griz dressed like the company in front of him.

Old Griz invoked the Creator and began his prayers with a blessing for the comfort and safety of the gathering and for 'the work' that would take place today. Old Griz called the parents forward with their three month old baby girl. Granny and Papa stood with them along with the aunt and uncle who, by prior agreement, would take care of their niece if the need arose. A new born had relatives chosen for them in case the parents died, at which time these relatives became the child's parents. This was a lifelong commitment. A child was never an 'orphan' in our culture.

Granny, being the matriarch and name giver, stepped forward and spoke quietly with Old Griz, whispering the name chosen for baby.

Old Griz stood in front of the group and offered prayers for the family and protection for baby. He spoke baby's name for the first time, as the proud parents held their precious bundle, secure and warm in her cedar root baby basket. The basket was beautifully imbricated with the family owned Snowflake design. Old Griz called forward the protective spirit of the name: "Hummingbird, we welcome you." The small group turned to the Four Directions, invoking baby's name at each turn. There was an audible sigh throughout the crowd in acknowledgement that it was a good name. At the time of baby's birth, Granny had seen a hummingbird, hovering over the first flowers of spring. Hummingbirds loved the high mountains of spring and summer. They were tiny but fierce when their nests were disturbed by a predator. "Joy Bringer" is the way the people thought of hummingbirds with their colourful feathers and protective spirit.

As soon as Hummingbird was able to crawl and move independently around her own hearth and begin to explore the living space around her, grandmothers and aunties would watch her to study where her interests were strongest. They would capture a child's natural curiosity and let them explore the space around themselves, until they were walking, and enlarging their spheres of interest. By the time Hummingbird was two years old her family would have an understanding of her nature and her interests. Hummingbird would never hear the harsh words: "no, don't do that", or "no don't touch." All children were distracted from causing themselves and others harm. Children were not shouted at or hit. All children were cherished. In this way of life, being fearful or stubborn was not acceptable.

In this culture of the survival of the fittest these were not helpful traits. Children were taught confidence by the modelling of their family and the community. Similarly, boys were watched over by family members, and would eventually learn the skills of their particular lineage, for example canoe building, plank making for the Longhouse, making nets for fishing, hunting, and many other skills. Each person's contribution to the skills and work needed to provide for their family and community was important. Everyone was aware of this today at this celebration.

Witnesses were called and came forward, the chiefs and leaders received a woven blanket or an animal pelt and others received a bandana with coins tucked into the corner. Witnesses were chosen to represent the different villages in the Territory, and all agreed that they would remember the naming and the events of the gathering. They also shared the story of the gathering with others who did not attend the event. Granny and the women brought out gifts to be distributed to the guests, oohs and ahhs were heard as each recipient graciously accepted his or her gift. The joy came from knowing that each gift was handmade by someone in the community.

At a signal everyone stood up as the Feast Song was rendered. Everyone present agreed that August was the best time for a gathering, the harvest had been generous this year as the array of fresh vegetables and berries showed, and the four legged were fat at this time of year too.

It was 'Feasting' time and the guests brought their own plates and bowls and cutlery. The youth of the community stepped up and began serving the elders. Long lines formed as each person waited for their turn to serve themselves. Serving tables groaned under the load of food that each one held, from the savoury meat stews to the barbeque salmon, roast moose and elk to the underground roasted potatoes.

Corn on the cob and other vegetables followed as well as the salad greens. The cooks had prepared granny's favourite dish, barbeque salmon heads, which she relished and gave it credit for her longevity. Granny always said this with a wink, but it always left one with the feeling that she meant it.

The feast wound down slowly as the guests enjoyed the food and each other's company and the warm sunny day with a gentle breeze riffling the leaves of the trees. Some of the elders dozed in the shade, the youth found activities to do; some went to the lake, skipping rocks across the surface of the water, others took a dip to cool off, a ball started a game. A 'Stick Game' was another pass time with a good prize for the winning team, and the audience cheered their favourites and groaned when their team got behind and so it went all afternoon.

The evening's activities began with a drum roll, capturing everyone's attention. Greetings and recognition were given to visiting leaders and guests were welcomed once again. The 'Welcome Song' was sung and the social dances began. After a round of songs, attention was given to the young woman who had come of age during the year.

Blue Thunderbird Sky Dancer had performed her rituals properly in accordance with custom. She had gone out to a secluded place, which had been used for this purpose for as long as any woman could remember. She went with her sponsor, her Auntie and several women. A small hut was ready for her. The young girl would use this hut for three or four months while she learned her duties and responsibilities. A girl sat in the hut unless she was called to work. She had to remain silent as well, always taking instructions. The only time a girl laid down was to sleep. Her sponsor, usually an aunty, was designated by Granny to teach the young girl.

A girl's first 'Moon Time' was significant and meant that she must leave the things of childhood behind. The women spent restful nights in the lodge close to the girl's hut. After breakfast, Auntie sat with her niece. She took her hands in hers and looked into her eyes until their connection was established.
Aunty said: "You are sacred and holy, and your body is sacred and holy, you are in your own ceremony." Every Aunty would say these words to her niece, generation after generation.
Aunty stood and picked up her makeshift broom to sweep the area around them. Aunty sat, and resumed her teaching. "Secondly," Aunty said, "in the hard times to come, you may not be able to be secluded during your moon time. You will need to put away your 'medicine bundle' and other instruments during this time and stay away from other ceremonies as well, remember that you are in your own ceremony."
The changes were foreseen by more than one Medicine Man and Medicine Woman who had the gift of looking through the veil and seeing the future of the people. "Child, you must remember these teachings, Granny will visit us tomorrow. She will ask you what you have learned and you must answer her. If Granny is satisfied with your words and actions you will receive the name chosen for you."
Toward the end of a young girl's confinement the women stayed by the fire under the light of the moon for several nights, giving instructions and teaching songs; every woman enjoyed sharing this time with a young woman who was preparing to be a 'Life Giver'.

As the sun rose in the morning the women bathed and dressed the new Life Giver in new clothes and waited for Granny's visit. Granny was satisfied with her granddaughter's lessons and thanked her caregivers for their teachings. Granny had the name ready. The women solemnly and reverently gathered round to hear the name chosen.
Granny said: "Your name is 'Blue Thunderbird Sky Dancer'. This name honours both sides of your lineage."

Blue Thunderbird Sky Dancer and her family had been busy for months preparing for her give away for this celebration. It was important that she'd show off her new skills; they showed that she had paid attention to the teachings of her elders.

Her first gift was for her teacher: Granny who had spent long winter hours showing her how to make cedar root baskets for which Granny was renowned. It was not her first basket because that one had mistakes and was not a suitable gift for her teacher. Blue Thunderbird Sky Dancer chose to make a berry picking basket, not an easy choice for a first basket. As well as being symmetrical it needed to be water proof. Granny accepted the gift with tears of joy and gratitude and pride in the knowledge that basket making would continue after her lifetime.

Through this demonstration of Blue Thunderbird Sky Dancer's basket making skill, she had earned the right to carry on her family tradition and to use the family emblem in her work.

Blue Thunderbird Sky Dancer made other gifts, which she had sewn or beaded, these were supplemented by the generous donation of articles made by the women of the community. It was understood that Blue Thunderbird Sky Dancer would be married in three years time to the young man chosen for her when she was a baby. Alliances within the Territory and with neighbouring territories were strengthened in this peaceful manner. Her family lineage was one of leadership in the community. The family made careful note of her helpers in order to reciprocate in future gatherings. Reciprocity is a fundamental part of the culture.

The dates for future celebrations were announced and committed to memory and as the date approached a 'Runner' went from one village to another with the invitation reminder.

Granny looked around. The evening chores were done and there was time for telling a story and enjoying a cup of tea. It's was important to tell these young ones sitting at her feet stories of past events and people. The children waited expectantly for Granny to begin. The young voices clamoured for their personal favourites.
"Granny, tell the Flood story."
"Granny, tell us about The Transformer Beings."
"Granny, tell us about Laloya."

Granny shifted in her chair. She suddenly thought of her Sama7 friend Maude White. "Granny met Maude on a sunny spring day. We were both gathering fresh greens and mushrooms in the same meadow. We were young women, she was Maude and I was Keek-lok-ik. Now, my friend Maude is called Nana and I am Granny to everyone." Granny smiled as she said this. The children were young enough to giggle at the thought of Granny being anything else except their beloved grandmother. All of these youngsters remembered Granny bundling up the newest baby and placing the baby in the new cedar root basket. When they reached teething age Granny would sit with them and offer her little finger for the child to chew on. When they didn't feel good Granny sat with the baby on her plump lap and the child would feel Granny stroking a cheek or rubbing a back and bring comfort and healing. Granny was present when they began to toddle around, she guided them gently around and was firm when a child was in danger of harming themselves or someone else. None of the children present wished to disappoint Granny.

Granny re-collected her thoughts about her Sama7 friend Maude.
"Maude and I met in a meadow. As I said, I was gathering fresh spring greens. The Sama7 woman thought she was gathering food. Sadly she was not. The mushrooms were poisonous and the greens were wrong too. Granny took pity on the Sama7 woman. They did not speak each other's language so they began signing and gesturing and using the Trade Language called 'Chinook'. Even with that it was difficult to communicate. Keek-lok-ik pointed her hand to herself; Maude also said her name while pointing to herself to indicate who she was. They got the giggles trying to say each other's names. Keek-lok-ik began removing greens and mushrooms from Maude's food gathering basket. Bad mushrooms got a 'Tuc-ch', which means bad tasting or not good. Maude spontaneously emptied her basket and said: "Tuc-ch." They laughed and Maude studied the contents of Keek-lok-ik's cedar root food gathering basket, who removed the strap from her forehead and let the basket down. They examined the mushrooms together."

"Picking up the bad mushrooms and holding the good mushrooms, Keek-lok-ik mimed smelling them and turning them over, examining them closely, looking at the mushrooms, noting the smell of a good mushroom versus the bad. "Phew," Maude said and they laughed. Next they turned their attention to the dandelion greens. Maude's were old, they were bitter and milky. "Tuc-ch," they said together and laughed. They gathered roots and shoots and greens and good mushrooms all afternoon. A friendship began that long ago day."

The children all knew Maude/Nana. They loved her cookies. Their visits were important to all of them.
Over the decades they had shared similar experiences. Maude's children had been mid-wifed by Keek-lok-ik's relative. Annie was her name and she carried on the teachings of being a good midwife and had delivered more than 300 babies in her lifetime.

Granny began again. "My friend Maude came to our Homeland on a big moving house with many other children and adults. Maude was 14 years old. She came by herself." The children let out involuntary sounds of sadness. "Yes," Granny continued, "Maude came alone with a paper attached to her bundle. A stern looking couple stepped forward to claim her. Maude was now an Indentured Servant and would remain so for seven years to pay for her passage."

"All Maude knew from that day forward was back breaking work and poor food, with one day of rest every seventh day. Maude went to her church in the morning where she met her future husband, five years later. Maude was not allowed to marry unless her passage was fully paid, neither Maude nor her future husband could pay the amount owing, and so she remained indentured until the age of 21." Granny explained that her friend Maude was an orphan. Granny explained this to the children. "Maude had no family to look after her." She needed to explain this idea as the concept was new to the children around her. "Maude lived in a country called "Ng lund" (England) in a big city. Her parents both died in an epidemic. Maude was left alone to scavenge and steal in the alleys and was caught stealing a loaf of bread and put on the big floating house (ship) to the West Port on the island of our homeland. Maude and her husband cleared many acres and built a cabin and a barn for the milk cow and pigs; they also had chickens and a large kitchen garden." The children looked at Granny in dismay and sorrow for those far way children who had no one to look after them. Granny continued: "Each of you know that if anything bad happened to your parents, that you would be looked after by your relatives who stood with your parents on your naming day." Each child present made happy sounds of thanksgiving and joy that they had family to look after them. "Someday when you are grown up you will be asked to be the Guardian of a baby on his or her naming day. It is important for you to learn the skills of survival and skills of your family lineage." Each little head nodded in happy agreement.

The drums began and Granny sat for a few moments longer in reverie. "The meadow where she and Maude had met those many decades ago had been several days walk from the village of i 'istkena where Keek-lok-ik and her husband had spent the winter months living with her family. The Territory extended to the borders of the Sechelt people and was a trade route and a place where people shared the news and kept the treaties strong by marriage alliances. The Sechelt relatives were feeling the first brunt of strangers moving into their territory."

"It had been good to feel the first rays of sunlight while walking toward the ocean and getting off the plateau. The istken had many benefits; it was built into the earth at a depth that insured an even temperature and was efficient to heat. But it was cramped, the living space minimal. Keek-lok-ik and her husband enjoyed living with various members of the family and sharing the food that had been collected since last spring." Granny thought of her ancient relative Laloya who had given her life in an istken similar to this one, so that her people would live. "Kukwstum'ck acw

Kika, thank you Laloya," she thought. "The Ucwalmicw had lived in i 'istkena, since time immemorial. One summer the men went out because of word that there were strangers with weapons in the territory and no women travelling with them meant one thing: war. The women were left in the village to tend the community garden. On a bright summer day the women were tending to the garden when Laloya saw something shining by a large rock near the river, not too far from the garden. Laloya sounded the alarm and the women knew that they had to make it to the old istken, run up the ladder to safety and pull the ladder up in order to be safe. Laloya made sure that all the women were safe and she ran to the istken and started to go up the ladder when she felt a hand grab her and pull her down, she quickly told the woman at the top to pull the ladder up and run. Laloya looked at her attacker, he was a Spaniard, bronzed from the sun and life on the floating houses (ship), and dark as the mahogany used on these floating houses. He wore dingy canvas pants cut off at the knees and held together with twined rope. The shiny knife was not in his mouth any longer. He ravaged Laloya as did his mates. Laloya died that day, still a girl, as she had not begun her Moon Cycle. She died and is the bravest woman ever born to our people." Granny grinned to herself thinking of the social dancing that had begun and here she was thinking of her long dead ancestor. "Ah," she thought, "that is the way of things, the old ones remember."

The drums continued on through the wee hours of the night, it was a memorable occasion.

2   *Granny & Papa*

Ol' Griz sat by the fire under the stars, enjoying the quiet sounds of the night, adding a log to the fire now and then. The old man reflected on his great grandson's comment early this morning. This morning as they were doing camp chores together, the little boy suddenly said: "Great Papa, I want to be just like you when I grow up." Ol' Griz hid his surprise by continuing to stack wood on the woodpile. Little Hawk was almost six years old. He asked questions from morning to night. Ol' Griz thought that he would wait until after the hunting trip to speak to Little Hawk's family about taking him on as an apprentice.

This year's hunting camp was located beside the river. They were a little bit early this year, so a few chips of fresh cut wood were added to the camp fire to create smoke and a gentle breeze kept the mosquitoes and flies away. Hunting camp sites were rotated frequently to prevent the over use of the land and resources, giving the land time to replenish itself. The ancestors had left this message with the people: "Be good Caretakers of Mother Earth."

The Ucwalmicw had learned and passed down the stories of the Shape Shifters, who had passed through the territory in the long distant past. The Shape Shifters had brought the gifts of the land, water, and air to the people, in the gift of cedar and the knowledge of cedar's many purposes. They had brought the salmon and other fish to the lakes, rivers and streams, the four legged ones and the winged ones. The Shape Shifters taught the people to be good caretakers; by being good caretakers the people would always have the resources to prepare for winter, and so it was and remained until the strangers entered the territory. It was then that things began to change, and not for the betterment of the people.

The outline of old drying racks was visible and rebuilt. The rack for stretching hides was also repaired and ready for use. The preparations were completed earlier that day. It was now time to relax until Ol' Griz had a dream showing him that the elk and mountain sheep were moving down the mountain for the wild hay and oats to fatten up for the long cold winter months. Ol' Griz kept his vigil through the night in a light sleep, waiting for the animals to show him where they were in the Dreamtime. Another day dawned. After breakfast the women went out berry picking and collecting the herbs which would be made into remedies for winter ailments.

Ol 'Griz settled himself by the fire once again, waiting for the dreamtime message from the animals. As he fell asleep, instead of dreaming of the hunt, he found himself sitting with his Spirit Guide. His Spirit Guide had come with him on the day of his birth and had shown himself at various times with important messages. He held his sacred pipe in the crook of his arm. His Spirit Guide spoke, he said:

"Tomorrow will bring change into your life. You will once again become a teacher to a young boy." Ol' Griz greeted the dawn with prayers on his lips as he had done throughout his long life.

The people in camp rose at dawn. They were expectantly waiting for O' Griz to tell them of the dreamtime and where the animals were. Ol' Griz knew the hunters were ready and eager to set out on the mountain trails. Ol' Gris admitted to having a dream but it was not the one he expected to have. The people were disappointed that the hunt would not begin that day.

Suddenly, Little Hawk took his Great Papa's hand excitedly: "Great Papa, I had a dream last night. I dreamed that the elk and mountain goats have moved down the mountain, over that way," he pointed to the mountain, "over there," he pointed again. Ol' Griz took time to consider his dream and the message. He turned to the assembled camp, placing Little Hawk in front of himself with both hands on Little Hawk's shoulders. He announced that the hunt would begin just as Little Hawk had described. A sigh and a cheer went up as Ol' Griz said prayers for a safe and successful hunting season and for his and Little Hawk's new roles, and that he would have time to teach the young boy. The old man had already decided to speak with the parents after the hunt.

As the first rays of sunlight appeared, family members stood aside to allow the hunters to check their gear. The horses were saddled and pack horses loads adjusted. Carelessness and sloppy preparation were not an option in these rugged mountains. A careless slip of any kind could mean serious trouble. The mountains are awesome and majestic, weather conditions changed quickly.

These were experienced hunters who knew and understood their territory intimately and knew how to read the signs left by wildlife and weather conditions. The hunters set out and looked forward to the adventure they were sure to have.

A cold nose touched his cheek waking the hunter instantly. 'Golobo' was the dog's name; he was the best hunting dog in the village. The hunter listened and felt that it was too quiet. The dog went to the other hunter and nudged him as well. Instantly alert, the men rolled out of their bedrolls, rifles in hand. Similarly, the hunters woke their young charges who understood from an early age to keep silent when awakened. The dog was standing, facing out from the camp with his neck ruff standing straight up. There were several possibilities. They were in bear and cougar territory. They quickly reasoned that it was summer with plenty of food available to the large predators. They could not catch an animal scent in the air, and thought the animal was making his way to drink at the river or if it was a bear to feast on salmon. The camp fire was rekindled, water boiled and leaves added to brew tea. Even in summer the mountain range was cool at this time of morning. The hunters patted each young man's shoulder in assurance that they had conducted themselves well. The men opened their cache and ate a small amount of food. It was an accepted custom to eat sparingly when hunting. The small group quickly and quietly mounted their horses for the ride over to the meadow. Past the meadow was a bluff with a snow melt stream where deer came to drink after leaving their sleeping nests. The hunters left the horses near the bluff and walked toward the creek. The deer came forward. The buck deer were in the background. The hunters signalled the young boys to get ready. They did. Each boy found his target and fired. Clean shot was signalled by each hunter. The young boys had proven their hunting ability today. The mature hunters watched as each boy realized what he had accomplished. The hunters turned their attention to the work at hand. Hanging, skinning, and cleaning the deer meat, being careful not to damage the hide which their proud mama's would tan for many uses.

Old Smitty, ever vigilant to the sound of gun shots, heard two distant pops, which meant that the young boys had been successful in their first hunt. His usually dour countenance grew animated as he smiled and got the camp cooks busy for the return of the small group of hunters. There was the hum of excitement as families prepared to welcome the young men. Smitty began to work with the cooks as a helper when he was a young boy. Smitty was one of the rare boys who could not tolerate the killing of any animal, or the violent actions of learning to be a warrior and he was not fond of being out of camp; it was his way. He had found his place, building the cooking fires, cutting wood, lifting and carrying heavy loads. Smitty learned to cook with the cast iron pots and pans which the gold miners had left behind. He was an asset to the camp. In the depth of winter Smitty would paint his face white to become a clown. He told stories through miming the actions of community members or acting out stories of myths and legends. The community welcomed these distractions in the midst of snow storms and blizzards that would keep everyone indoors for many days or occasionally, for weeks.

Two specially chosen hunters left camp on the first day of encampment. A third man rode with them as far as the horses could safely travel. The man and horses returned to base camp. After several days the man would return with the horses to the base of the mountain and keep vigil for the hunters return. The hunters now on foot, made their way along old trails, passing familiar markers on the trail on the mountain. The alpine meadows were ablaze with colour and activity at this time of year. Bees buzzed the air flitting from one flower to another, gathering nectar. The hunters had been watching and waiting for this. They patiently scanned the area watching the bees in flight. The hunters spied the hive's location at the same time. The hive was in the hollow of a tree about twenty feet from the ground. All their skills and knowledge were tested and used if they were going to be successful in this year's bear hunt. The men set aside their bedrolls, covering them with leaves and settled down to wait for the bear to find the honey tree. At dusk the men prepared a sleeping place.

On the morning of the third day the hunters woke up feeling hopeful that the day's sunshine would bring the bear to find his favorite treat, honey. The hunters left their sleeping place, checking the breeze and finding a spot to take up their watchful vigil. At mid morning the hunters were alerted to the noisy caw of birds on the opposite side of the hill, where a mature, healthy looking black bear was making his way to the honey tree. The bear had possibly made this trek with his mother as a cub. The hunters gave a sigh of relief when they saw the male bear. A female bear with a cub would mean that the hunters would have a long trek ahead of them to the other known honey tree.

The hunters waited patiently, keeping downwind of the bear. The bear was intent on the aroma of the honey. At the base of the honey tree the bear began to climb. The hunters waited until the bear reached into the hive, they raised their rifles and one hunter made the heart shot while the other waited to make sure the bear was dead and fell to the ground. The agitated bees flew madly about and began repairing the damage to the hive. The hunters moved forward with a pitch covered torch creating smoke so that they could move the dead bear. Once the bear was moved a safe distance from the honey tree the hunters turned the bear's head to the West and said a prayer for the spirit of the bear and to give thanks for a successful hunt. The men threw ropes over the branch of a tall tree and hauled the bear up so that they could dress it out. While it was taboo for the people of the territory to eat bear meat, it was not taboo to take the whole hide, skinning the bear for the fat to be rendered down by the women while still fresh. The men worked skilfully and quickly, leaving the carcass for other animals to feed on. The men made a travois and each carried part of the load. They stopped only once to strip off their clothing to jump into the glacial mountain lake with a whoop and a holler at the cold water. They continued on until dusk, hanging their burden in a tree and making a small fire, while one man slept and the other kept watch in two hour shifts. They awoke very early, anxious to rejoin their families.

The look- out smiled and was happy that he had brought fresh horses and food for the men from Old Smitty whose instincts told him to prepare food to send with the lookout. The men were welcomed back to the community. The community would benefit from the grease which would be used in countless ways throughout the winter. The cooks turned their energy to preparing a feast for the community and the returning hunters. It was a great feast. The people sat by the fire in small family clusters waiting for the story telling time to begin. Each hunter told his story of the hunt and was acknowledged. The two young hunters received their community's cheers and they beamed with pride.

It was always a Grandmother who told the First Deer Story. "At the dawn of remembrance," she began, "animals and humans understood each other. The people were starving. First Deer spoke to First Hunter and said: "We, the Deer Nation, love and take pity on you two legged ones. We see that you are hungry, approach us in a good manner, wishing to feed yourself and others and we will stop and turn our head toward you, that you may spear us." First Deer and First Hunter made contact with the spear point. A sacred message was transmitted to

First Hunter through a stream of consciousness. First Hunter relayed the message from First Deer: "Use every part of my body to nourish yourself and others, my hide to clothe yourself and others and eat my marrow to give you strength." All of the necessary information was passed along to First Hunter and was passed along through the millennium to the present time."

Grandmother's storytelling had the desired affect; the people were relaxed and ready for a good night's sleep and making their way to their winter homes.

3   *Granny & Papa*

Ol' Griz is tending the sacred fire. His family is gathered, they are honouring his request for this special meeting. Ol' Griz adds cedar shavings to the wood and lights the fire. He begins his prayers by offering pinches of pungent wild sage. He invokes the Creator and the Keepers of the Four Directions and the Four Winds. He offers prayers to the unseen Spirits and to the ancestors and he remembers his late wife. Ol' Griz takes time to think of their early years together and the family they made, saddened by the thought of the epidemic that took her life while she cared for others.

Today is a celebration of his great grandson Little Hawk. Ol' Griz gives thanks for the blessings and abundance that the Territory has provided for the Ucwalmicw this year. Ol' Griz gives silent thanks to his nephew at Cayooshe Creek for the sage. He had traded devil's club, which was plentiful here, for the sage in the plateau area of the territory. Ol' Griz looks around the circle of his sons, grandson and sees Little Hawk. Great Papa motions to Little Hawk to come close. Little Hawk is very excited, but does his best to imitate his elders by standing quietly and respectfully. Great Papa looks around at each adult man present. He continues: "Each of you had your special day within this group." The adult men nod their heads in agreement. "It is our custom to observe a child from birth to about two years of age. We watch their progress, observing their interests and activities." The men nod and smile their agreement and so do the women sitting at the back of the circle. The women are sitting at the outside of the circle in case their attention is needed elsewhere, they don't wish to be disruptive.

Great Papa reminds the group that Little Hawk has said that he wishes to follow in his footsteps. Great Papa turns to his grandson, Little Hawk's father.
"What have you observed?" he asks.
"Little hawk has followed you around since he could crawl. He followed you to your swimming place since he was two years old, and wept until you carried him into the water with you. Great Papa, you created a safe place for the boy to swim with you each new dawn, all seasons of the year. At this years' hunt Little Hawk had the dream showing him where the animals were in the mountains, you gave your blessings and we had a successful hunt."
"Little Hawk has a special gift. Our concern is for you, Great Papa. Little Hawk's training is longer than any other."

Ahh, Ol' Griz thought, perhaps the time has come to speak of the dream I had. During the recent hunt we all witnessed Little Hawk's demonstration of his dreamtime. We followed that hunting trail. I had been waiting for the animals to show themselves to me. Great Papa looked around himself and said: "My Spirit Guide came to me that night with this message: "Your life will change once again as you again become a teacher to a young boy." My Spirit Guide has always prepared me for the next step in my journey. So it is, and with your permission and his mothers' I am ready to begin this journey with Little Hawk." This was uttered with great affection and emotion.

Little Hawk's parents stood proudly behind their son. Great Papa put out his hands and Little Hawk joined him. "You are not a baby any more, today you choose to undertake your training as my apprentice, do not be afraid Little Hawk, we will continue as we have been. Today you will join me at my cabin." Great Papa went on to explain that Little Hawk's gift of clairvoyance and in the dreamtime, meant that he needed guidance to become disciplined, and to recognize the sign posts and false faces in the dreamtime, he would learn the spiritual language. Little Hawk was also 'empathic'; this meant that he picked up on other people's thoughts and feelings. He would learn to tell the difference between his own feelings and those of others. "This trait is important to understand," he explained.

"Times are changing," Great Papa continued. "The Sama7 people come among us with their strange language and customs. Little Hawk and I discussed this with his parents. We are in agreement that the boy will be kept away from these strangers until he is grown." Everyone present nodded agreement. "Already, the Sama7 people are showing that they are lazy to learn our language and are trying to change us." Other children would make this transition from babyhood to young boys and girls throughout the year.

The adults were looking forward to the training. The games the children played would teach them many things .Dexterity, speed, patience, co-operation with others. Spinning tops taught patience, dexterity with a sense of accomplishment when the top was spinning. These tops were made of cedar wood. The boys always challenged each other to foot races, tree climbing, rock throwing, and in countless other ways. Adults were watchful. Competition is healthy but being unfair in a contest was greatly frowned upon.

Children also received a paddle at this time, sized to fit and maple wood being the best choice. The children paddled around in small canoes close to the shore. The boys received a cured hard wood staff. This staff had many uses. It was used in warrior training, but not as a weapon against each other. The adults demonstrated the staff's uses as a defensive weapon; later when the boys grew stronger at this game black soot was mixed with grease which was added to one end to simulate a spear. A drummer, singer would sing the warrior's actions in a battle or on the hunt. The warrior would demonstrate his actions with his spear or war club. The drum set the pace of the demonstration. The young boys watched and later practiced the movements, always striving to do their best. A stealth game was played as well to teach the young ones patience and self control. Skills and interests had also been observed by the adults.

The young girls were having their ceremonies as well and also hearing that they were no longer babies. Their potential skills and interest had also been observed by the adults. The girls gravitated to an auntie or older cousin or granny and would apprentice with her in her area of expertise.

For some girls cedar root basketry was like a magnet and they would spend many happy hours with being helpful to Granny as she sat with a basin of water in front of her and various roots, sticks, cherry bark and grasses were used. Again, the teaching took the form of a game. A child learned and named each part and tool used in the process. Granny's smile was something the child strived for and was rewarded with generously. In season, the girls went out cedar root digging, food collecting, greens early in the spring, hak wa7, dandelion leaves while young and tender, stinging nettles, salmon berry leaves and blackberry leaves and other greens. The roots of Ferns which grew on the giant maple tree trunks, a sweet treat and refreshed the breath too. Older girls learned about mushroom picking. The smell of wood land mushrooms of various kinds were picked from early spring until late in the fall. Every woman looked forward to these treats in her kitchen. If a warrior or hunter was high enough in the mountains he could bring back a sack full and the bounty was shared.

Girls were also given a paddle and there was always a small canoe available to use, while they also paddled close to shore. Girls learned to clean and prepare salmon and other fish, including sturgeon, which lived in the river, but made their way to the bay in Harrison Hot Springs in the summer months. Smoked sturgeon is a real delicacy in the winter months. Berry picking season is an awesome time in a child's life. Grannies and Aunties carried large cedar root berry picking baskets on their backs. The baskets were held in place by a strap which was long enough to place comfortably around the forehead and held in place, so that a berry picker could pick a handful of berries and cast them directly into the basket. The child, "not being a baby any more" filled her small basket before eating any berries. Gathering food for winter use is very important. As young as these children were, they already understood the concept of doing their part in food gatherings as well as doing their share of chores.

Ol' Griz in his capacity as both medicine man and leader of his people understood that his family needed this time of reflection, he quietly added a few pinches of sage to the fire. He thought that tomorrow, he would bring out the alder hoops he had requested to be made for the boys and girls. It would give the children pleasure and the exercise would be good for them. He recalled his days of standing a hoop on edge and getting it moving and the fun of the chase, the fun of chasing after it while keeping it in motion. He would bring out the child size stilts as well. He smiled at the thought of the families sitting around in the sunshine enjoying the antics of their small relatives, testing their speed and agility, not to mention staying upright on the stilts.

The head cook waved, which was a signal that the feast was ready. Ol' Griz stood up and spoke to his family. "Today we have set and accepted Little Hawk's and my new pathway. We understand the reasons for the boy to come and live with me, away from distractions. Little Hawk must learn the skills that all boys learn for survival; he must learn the Spiritual language, the names of places and identify plants and medicines, he must learn to drum the songs, and learn to sing. In due time, the boy will walk out for his first night on the mountain. He will learn to connect with the Universe. "Enjoy your time with your family, Little Hawk, you and I will begin our journey when the first snow comes."

The family shared the meal together. Everyone was aware of the time remaining until winter set in. Ol' Griz smiled again, knowing that Little Hawk would be at the swimming place bright and early next morning. He felt the familiar tug of pride and gratitude for this small brave child.

4   *Granny & Papa*

Ol' Griz lifted his head as though listening to some invisible force. He received the message from the Spirit World; it was time to make his way to his holy place high up in the alpine meadow he had used all his life. He would spend the night and wait for a vision or dream to guide him.

Ol' Griz walked out of the village. The leaves were on the ground and there was frost on the ground every morning. His grandson would be tending the sacred fire close to his cabin. Ol' Griz wore his outdoor clothes and boots and a knitted sheep wool sweater and a knitted toque. He carried some tobacco to make offerings. Ol' Griz walked across the field toward the creek, across the foot bridge and disappeared behind the giant maple trees. It was a steep and rocky climb to the farthest point on Blueberry Mountain. The path was a familiar one. Ol' Griz was in good physical health and took time to look at the landmarks along the trail. It was always wise to be vigilant when out in the bush. There were large predators at this altitude and the old man watched for scat and tree markings which would tell him if there was bears or cougars nearby. Ol' Griz arrived at his sacred place. It was undisturbed. The balsam tree he liked to camp under was beside the mountain stream that was clear as crystal. Ol' Griz offered his prayers before collecting tree branches to spread on the ground which would be his resting place.

Ol' Griz was grateful for the small sweat house behind his cabin where he had voiced his question to the Spirit World last evening. It was early afternoon and Ol' Griz took off his outer clothes and dipped a tree branch into the stream and touched the wet branch to his shoulders and arm and drew it down one side of his body and then did the same thing to the other side of his body. He dipped the branch over his back repeating the motion. Then he cupped his hands in the icy water and washed his face and hands, knowing that this would acclimatize him quickly and also remove more of the human smells so that he could better blend in with nature. Ol' Griz then spread a small amount of sage around the sleeping area. Ol' Griz dressed once again and began offering his prayers, asking permission of the Great Spirit to be in this sacred place. He sat in his place with his back against the tree trunk enjoying the autumn sunshine. He concentrated on the sound of water running over the rocks in the glacial mountain stream to clear his mind and quiet his spirit.

It was dark and the temperature had dropped considerably. Ol' Griz changed position and drew warmth from the sacred fire far below him at his sweat house. After taking a few deep breaths Ol' Griz was in the dream time. He heard, "hello grandson." He stood up and smiled as he recognized his lifelong Spirit Guide. It was a good feeling being greeted in this manner. "Come grandson, let us begin our journey. We will begin our journey with your teachers and your family. You will review the steps in your learning and visit with your loved ones." Ol' Griz saw himself as a small child with his parents and surrounded by the community as he passed through his ceremony; from babyhood to young boyhood.

As the memories passed quickly, Ol' Griz felt the love and warmth which had surrounded him during his formative years. The images of his family faded, Ol' Griz knew that this was a gift. He would not see his loved ones again until it was his time to travel the western trail to the stars.

Ol' Griz recognized the place where he and his Spirit Guide were, it was familiar to them. They sat in a circle with other spirit elders. It was time to review the journey he and Little Hawk would be undertaking together. The spirit entities sent their information to Ol' Griz telepathically.

The main elements were the changes that the Sama7 had brought which were already having an impact on the people, such as moving from the collective way of living in the long houses and istken. The move to living in individual family dwellings was not efficient, they were too hard to heat, needing more resources to heat and cook meals. Other changes were coming. Many more of the strangers would come, imposing themselves and their way of life on the people.

In the beginning the strangers would trade fairly with the people but that would deteriorate. Ol' Griz saw the greed for the land and its resources stripped away, leaving nothing for the original people. The hopelessness and despair would begin when the black robed men arrived. They would build structures on the landscape. The purpose of these structures was for the orphans, who were alone because of the epidemics of illness, such as measles, flu, and smallpox to mention a few. Later, all children were forced into attendance in these places. Great pain and suffering followed as parents and children were systemically torn apart. Ol' Griz viewed the landscape of the future, it was stripped of the trees, the gold, silver and copper ore were mined and the rivers once full of salmon were barren. The strangers made lines on the ground and claimed the land for themselves. His Spirit Guide spoke: "You and your children, grandchildren and Little Hawk were born free; soon the Sama7 people will overtake our nations."

His Spirit Guide brought Ol' Griz to the near future, showing him Little Hawk's progress to adulthood. Ol' Griz was pleased with the vision. Little Hawk would earn his name in time to come. He would have a long and happy life.

The Morning Star appeared and there was reverent silence as the birds and animals hushed. Ol' Griz gave thanks to his Spirit Guide and those who had joined them in the sacred circle. He also understood that this was his last visit to this sacred place in this lifetime. He made his offerings of tobacco in thanksgiving for the vision. He stepped out of this sacred circle and made his way down the mountain to his small sweat house where his grandson greeted him with a nod. After his cleansing sweat he shared a feast with his family. The only information he volunteered about his time on the mountain was to assure them that all would come to pass.

Little Hawk's eyes danced and sparked as he stepped out and saw that it was snowing. He had been waiting for this day. They walked to the swimming hole and broke the ice and jumped in. This ritual was practiced daily. Smitty brought the tea and food, a task he would carry out daily, he also made sure that there was plenty of wood split, as Little hawk was too young to do this as yet. A winter time routine was established, and would vary according to Little Hawk's abilities, he was already willing to take on tasks that were clearly out of his reach. Great Papa smiled.

5   Ol' Griz

Ol' Griz, Little Hawk and Smitty heard the 'Watchman' approach the village from the trail at the back of the cabin. He was the last one to return from his lookout point high up in the mountain range on the west side of the valley. There were several feet of snow in the mountains. It was now impossible for anyone, friend or foe, to get through. The other Watchmen had been returning within a day or two of each other with a cache of moose or elk meat on a rough built sled. The lone Watchman trudged through the snow, bundled up and wearing his snow shoes. He was warmly greeted with hot tea and food. Smitty went to the sled and removed some of the fresh frozen meat from the sled. He thanked the Watchman who would then go on to deliver the rest of the meat to those who had not received any as yet. At last he had finished his work for this season and would enjoy his family and community for a few months.

When the Watchman had left to join his family, Smitty sharpened his knives in preparation to cutting into the frozen bounty of fresh meat. Smitty stoked up the fire and put the cast iron pan on the stove and began cutting slivers of meat. He put grease into the hot pan with a few wild onions and dropped the meat into the pan. The meat sizzled and cooked and filled the cabin with wonderful aromas. Ol' Griz offered up prayers of thanksgiving for the Watchmen who performed this duty for the people annually. Throughout the village similar rituals were taking place and feasting was being enjoyed by everyone. The remainder of the frozen meat was cached outside, safe from the dogs and, as winter progressed, from predators, hungry enough to come close to the village because of hunger.

Little hawk was full and feeling drowsy. He wanted Papa to tell him a story. Little Hawk had turned six and was full of questions.
Today, the question was: "Papa what does 'time immemorial' mean?"
His papa chuckled deep within himself, careful not to show this outwardly. Smitty busied himself with the cleanup from the feast. When Little Hawk realized that Papa was going to answer his question, he sat up straight to demonstrate his alertness, this being also a sign of respect for the storyteller.

Papa gathered his thoughts.
He began, "time immemorial means that it is the way we have done things, generation after generation." Papa chose his words carefully because he knew that it was important, for Little Hawk's understanding. "Little Hawk," he said, "we have lived in these holy mountains since time immemorial, meaning that Kal' kuc'pi placed us here to be care takers of this land, the water, the animals, the birds, the plants and trees and all of the resources that we use."

Ever ready with a question or comment, Little Hawk said: "But Papa, we cut trees to make our canoes and build houses, we catch the salmon and animals to eat." Papa looked at his great grandson with astonishment, and thought that perhaps he had posed the same thoughts and ideas to his teachers.

Papa continued: "at the beginning of time when Kal' kuc'pi placed us here he gave us the gifts of plenty and all things that we needed. Since time immemorial we have used the resources given to us, not taking more then we could use or share with our relatives. It is our sacred duty to do this. It also means that you will pass on the knowledge and skills that you are being taught to the next generation."

Little Hawk looked deeply into Papa's eyes with the silent promise that he would do his best to fulfill his part in 'time immemorial'. Papa smiled and patted his shoulder.

Smitty banked the fire and he went to his sleeping place. Papa watched Little Hawk as he got into his bed. Their beds were close together. This was comforting to the little boy. Papa offered up his last thoughts in prayer. Ol' Griz prayed for the people, and prayed that Little Hawk would sleep well, without the troubling dreams; he understood that 'dreams of future events' was possible for the young boy, but he hoped not, not just yet.

At dawn, midway through the winter months, Smitty was building the fire in preparation to cooking. Ol' Griz and Smitty began a conversation about going to the Tsek. The Tsek is a sacred place to the people. It is where hot water bubbles up from the ground, and where glacially cold water flows beside it. The morning swimming holes that they used daily were frozen over solid. There were several factors to consider. Firstly, did they have enough food to share with the couple who lived there in a house made by the Sama people, who had passed through this way on their way to the gold trails? Was there enough wood stock-piled for them to use for the remainder of the winter? Smitty assured his relative that there was enough to meet all of their needs.

The men discussed using the istken. They both thought that it would be a good experience for Little Hawk. Smitty had checked the istken's readiness to be used when he was there in the autumn. When it stopped snowing, Smitty left the cabin to go to invite the family to come and hear the proposed plans. The family arrived and had tea while they listened to Ol' Griz. He spoke of the plans to move to the Tsek for the balance of the winter months. Help was quickly offered and accepted.

Two large Percheron horses were harnessed and a sled was brought forward and hooked up. The air was cold and formed clouds of breath from the horses and people. Staples and household necessities were strapped onto the sled, Ol' Griz and Smitty sat with Little Hawk between them. They sat on a bale of hay which would later feed the horses, nothing was wasted, a small bag of oats was set aside to feed the horses, so that they would not be a burden to the couple who lived at the Tsek.

Little Hawk's father clicked his tongue and the horses and the sled moved forward. It was not a great distance to travel, just a few miles. They were all aware of the weather and the swiftly running stream that they needed to cross, half-way to their destination. They were in luck; when they arrived at the stream, it was partially frozen. This was important and made it easier to cross over. The horse team steadied and kept up a good pace. They arrived at The Tsek, and were warmly greeted by their hosts. Steaming cups of devil's club tea were offered and gratefully enjoyed by all before unloading the sled.

Kindling wood was ready in the small fire pit. It had been left by the last occupants who had stayed there. Ol' Griz lit the fire in the istken while others unloaded the sled. They fed and rested the horses. News was exchanged and messages relayed to family members living in Samahquam. It was time for the return journey, before the weather changed. Little Hawk waved at his father as the horse team and sled turned and started for home.

Little Hawk was excited and happy at the turn of events. While his relatives were busy organizing the living area and putting away the staples of food, Little Hawk sat and watched his elders, contently. Soon the istken was warm and cozy and a cast iron pot was bubbling with ts'wan, dried wild onions and dried wild potatoes. Fresh cedar boughs were cut and placed at each person's sleeping place and covered with a thick ticking of straw.

Papa picked up his drum and began to sing. Little Hawk joined in with his little boy voice, high pitched and clear. Papa and Smitty smiled, they knew that in a few short years the boy's voice would take on the deep resonance of his father's. His father was renowned for his singing and drumming, he was especially welcome to sing when the 'stick games', slahal, was played.

After singing and drumming for a time, Smitty said that their meal was ready. They ate with relish, slurping up the juice left in their bowls. After a short rest, Papa playfully asked Little Hawk if he would like to take a bath in the dugout tub of hot water. Little Hawk was ready to join in whatever papa wanted to do. Smitty carefully added cold water to the steaming hot sulphurous water and they got in. Papa carefully explained to the boy that a person didn't stay in the water too long, as the water lost the beneficial effects. When they got out of the water in about a half hour, papa showed Little Hawk how to scrub his body with the snow; he was reluctant until papa explained that the snow would cool him down. Smitty got in the tub and when he was ready to get out, he rolled around in the snow making the boy laugh. Little Hawk did this too after each daily bath. All of them were happy and relaxed when they returned to the istken.

Smitty's sleeping place was on one side of the fire pit, while Papa and Little Hawk shared a space on the opposite side. The two men spoke about the need to begin the boy's training in the dreamtime. This must be undertaken carefully and slowly. Papa explained to Little Hawk that he would be connecting with him in the dreamtime to begin transmitting the history of the Ucwalmicw.
"This," he explained further,"is the purest way for you to receive the information."
He went on, "My Spirit Guide will come, he will introduce himself to you and when you are spiritually connected he will begin giving you the information. I will be with you," he said.
Little Hawk listened carefully and nodded his head in agreement.
Then as always, he had a question. "Papa, who taught you when you were growing up?"
Papa blinked his surprise and answered, "my Great Papa."
"Who taught him?" the little boy persisted.
"His Papa taught him," Ol' Griz answered.
The little boy's eyes sparkled with insight and he said, "Papa is that what 'time immemorial' means?" "Yes," he said.
He and Smitty shared a smile over the boy's head in silent agreement that this small boy would keep them busy answering his questions.

And so it began, each night Papa became Ol' Griz, the teacher, and they began their journey, connecting with each other in the dreamtime. Faces and places were a jumble at first but Little Hawk was eager to learn and soon sorted out his feelings and setting them aside.
Ol' Griz' Spirit Guide came and said "Hello Grandson."
Little Hawk asked the stranger in surprise: "How did you know my name?"
"I know you and all of your history."
Little Hawk was comfortable. He saw another Spirit near papa's Spirit Guide.
"Who are you?" he asked.
"I am the one entrusted to your well-being since the moment you were born," he answered.
"What is your name?"
"When I was living among your people, a long time ago," he said, "I was called Warrior."
Little Hawk felt safe in the company of his Spirit Guide and the others here. This first venture into the spirit realm was successful. Little Hawk felt his body falling gently onto his bed and let out a small sigh.

Small groups from Skatin walked to The Tsek, wearing snow shoes. They came throughout the winter months to bathe and to visit. When it was required they asked respectfully for a healing from Ol' Griz, which he was always ready to give. Each person who received his help left a gift of food or other token of respect, perhaps chopping wood or making kindling. It is the way of our people.

Prior to the spring break-up Ol' Griz, Smitty and Little Hawk made their way home. The trails were impassable during spring break-up time. The rivers and streams were at full flood stage, and great care was taken in respect of this. No one took foolish chances, getting swept away by the raging waters.

The Watchmen took up their duties at various look out points in the high mountains. They returned to cabins or istken that dotted the landscape in these remote areas, some remnants still remain, as a silent testament to the brave men who did this unheralded service for the nation.

Little Hawk began learning skills that all boys must take part in. Each day he visited a relative to receive instruction. He had six summers to accomplish these necessary skills. He joined his other small relatives in paddling around in a small canoe. The boys found fun ways to challenge each other, as boys always seem to do.
The learning process was not a chore. Adults watched from the periphery taking pleasure in the antics of the children. Various disciplines were learned in the summer and Little Hawk gave all of his energy and skills to mastering each one. Great Papa/Ol' Griz relaxed his teachings at this time of year, because he understood that the exhaustion of physical activities of summer would ensure the boy would have deep restful sleep. And so it went for Little Hawk and his community.

He attended meetings with Ol' Griz in the village and also when Ol' Griz attended meetings within the Territory. Little Hawk was silent, listening respectfully to and memorizing the protocols of Leadership from his mentor and other respected leaders. Little Hawk remembered the time when Ol' Griz took him aside when he was asking too many questions.
"Little Hawk," he began, "do you know what happens when your mouth is open asking questions? Your ears are closed to hearing the answers."
Little Hawk remembered his reaction to this kindly delivered reprimand, he wriggled in embarrassment.

Later in the day, Ol' Griz lit a small fire with cedar shavings adding wood to the fire as needed. He called Little Hawk to come near. The boy trotted over.
"Little Hawk," he inquired, "do you know what happens to this wood when the fire goes out?"
He shook his head and waited for the answer that was sure to come.
"When the ashes are cold, we set them aside to sprinkle on the ground so that other things can grow."
Ol' Griz continued: "the sacred cedar tree continues to give to us even when it is burned to ashes."
Little Hawk's eyes rounded in wonder and understanding of this new information. He would cherish the memory of this lesson all of his life.

On another day, Little Hawk had a stick and was mindlessly striking a small frog when Papa came by. "What are you doing Little Hawk?" he asked. Little Hawk dropped the stick with a startled yip. He watched as Papa changed from papa to Ol' Griz the teacher. He waited. Ol' Griz looked a little disappointed in his actions.

"Little Hawk, you must not hurt any small creatures, everything has a place and a job to do, and this frog is your relative."
The boy looked at him in bewilderment.
Ol' Griz explained that Ucwalmicw are related to every other living thing on Mother Earth, and that all must be treated with respect. Thus began Little Hawk's understanding of: All My Relations.

The seasons came and went this way for the next four years adding knowledge and depth to Little Hawk's education and skills.

The people followed the rhythms and changes of the seasons, food gathering being the primary activity in the spring, summer and autumn.

Small children mimicked their older relatives when they went out gathering food. Children learned by observing an activity, being given small tools to fit their hands as they tried out new things. They were given encouragement by the adults present. The adult would model an activity and the child would try to do it. It was satisfying to the teacher and the child as well.

Ol' Griz called for a meeting of Little Hawk's family and community leaders.
"It is time for Little Hawk's time alone on the mountain for two nights."
He asked the people for their assessment of Little Hawk's readiness to undertake this test.
"It is important that Little Hawk is prepared in all aspects of his being. Is he physically strong? Is his mind good? Does he have the heart strength needed to be successful?"
"We have witnessed the boys' progress, Grandfather."
Each person gave his assessment of Little Hawk's ability and understanding of the necessary skills needed for survival. They were satisfied.

Ol' Griz looked about at the assembled group and said: "Little Hawk has been learning the spiritual language and is confident and fearless with good judgement for one so young. I believe that he is ready."
Little Hawk would undertake this test on the day before the longest day of summer. He still went for a daily swim, which helped to give him strength to withstand being alone on the hill and to avoid feeling hungry and thirsty while he was there.

It was time for cleansing and purification in the sweat house at the back of the cabin. They did this for four days with singing and drumming ringing out into the community. At dawn Little Hawk left the confines of the sweat house and began his hike to the place that his family had used for generations. Little Hawk was accompanied by his father and Ol' Griz, they went silently. Cedar boughs were brought to the site and laid down on the ground. It was hot during the day, but cold at night in the mountains so Little Hawk brought a blanket. His father surprised Little Hawk with a sea shell and sage and cedar that he had prepared for a smudge to ward off the mosquitoes and flies. He smiled his thanks. The adults left him.

Little Hawk, looked around at his surroundings feeling a thrill of vulnerability. The mound was on a hill in the high mountain overlooking the valley below where the village was and his family prayed for him. The mound was grassy and clear of brush. It gave Little Hawk a clear view all round himself. He laid the cedar boughs, arranging them soft side up and put his blanket on top. He took comfort in the knowledge that his father and Great Papa and countless generations had come here to pray for an answer to their questions. He settled himself on the cedar boughs, taking in deep breaths of the smell of the boughs.

Little Hawk looked at the vista around him, remembering how the hill looked from different directions. He heard an eagle screech in the distance in flight on the other side of the valley. Other birds were busy with nests and he noticed grasshoppers, ants and bees buzzing below. The familiarity of the landscape seen from here made him feel comfortable.

Little Hawk reached for his drum and began to sing, he sang four songs, he began his prayers. He spoke his prayers; asking the Universe to accept his being there. "I come in a peaceful manner, not to do anyone or anything harm," he said. "I come humbly, to connect with Kal Kuk'pi (Great Spirit), and my Spirit Guide and know him and hear his messages, I seek his knowledge."
He sang quietly and prayed throughout the day; it got cool and he drew his blanket around his body and fell asleep. The stars lighted the velvety night sky.

He felt a familiar presence, it was Papa's Spirit Guide, he stirred, and there was another Spirit presence, not quite so known but he felt safe. As he awoke in the dreamtime he saw his own Spirit Helper, Warrior.
"Come," he said, "let us go on a journey together."
Warrior scooped up the boy and put him on the neck ruffles of a very large white eagle.
"This is your sacred place and we will return to it remember it well. You must always return to your sleeping place after your journey." Little Hawk nodded agreement.

Warrior explained to Little Hawk that the pure white eagle was as ancient as the First Eagle who was placed on Mother Earth at the dawn of time. The boy noticed the long white whiskers under the eagle's beak, and was full of wonder that he was having this experience. He was given instruction: "you must always wait for this Ancient Eagle Helper to come to your aid when you are travelling in the Spirit World."

"This is a new sensation, the feeling of flying on an eagles' back, the feathers are so soft," he thought. "This is your first journey so we will fly over the valley and the village."
Little Hawk was full of amazement, the village was bright as day. He saw the houses and the cabin where he lived. Everyone was inside, with the exception of his

father and Great Papa who sat by the sweat house fire. LIttle Hawk heard his family singing and chanting and he heard them offering prayers for his well-being. During the day Smitty would keep the fire going, resting at night. The eagle flew further away to the mountain top and over it where Little Hawk could see the river and lakes and glacial streams below. They flew onward, making a wide arc over the territory. They continued onward toward the East, where Little Hawk noticed special markings on a jutting rock.
"Remember the markings," he was instructed, "these special markings have been left for travellers such as you. It will help you in the future when you have been on a very long journey, it will guide you safely back." Again the boy nodded. The eagle began the return journey to the cedar boughs. Little Hawk sat in wonder at all that he had witnessed. He greeted the Morning Star with prayers and gratitude and fell asleep. He had questions for his Spirit Helper, Warrior, but they would wait until later.

Day turned into night and Little Hawk was happy to see Warrior appear.
He asked: "When I was in the dreamtime, it was night. Why did the village look like daylight?"
Warrior answered: "Everything is possible in the Spirit World. The journey we are now taking is to the West. It is where the Kukwpi7 (Chief) of the Animals, our brother Bear lives, and he has called the four legged, winged ones and others to help to answer your question."

Again, he was lifted on the eagles' back and they flew in towards the West. When they arrived in the forest area, a really large bear was present with many other animals. The animals communicated with each other about the boy.
"He comes seeking the Medicine Way."
There were murmurs of interest among them.
"He is of strong lineage in these matters and has demonstrated his gifts to the benefit of the people at an early age. He is honest, patient, and willing to learn new skills."
"He comes with deepest respect to ask permission to begin learning the medicines on the land and how to use them," said Warrior, Little Hawk's Intercessor/Protector in this matter. The animals signalled the boy to move a small distance away. Warrior approached the boy reassuringly with the answer he was given.
"Yes, the Kukwpi7 (Chief) of Animals grants you permission to begin learning the medicine ways. Come now it is time to return to your cedar boughs." The boy slept.

Great Papa and his father came to the hill to bring Little Hawk to the sweat house, no words were spoken. They entered the sweat house and began their ceremony. After the first prayers were said, the adults looked at Little Hawk. It was time to tell of his experiences and so he did to these two most trusted people in his life. Deer broth was given to Little Hawk. Little Hawk's mother and the women of the community prepared a feast with Little Hawk's favourite foods which he relished after two days and two nights on the hill without either food or water. His mother had made him new moccasins as a gift.

Ol' Griz had been showing Little Hawk the medicine plants since he was a small boy. It was time to give him in depth teachings. Little Hawk would learn the name of the plant, where it grew, when to harvest it and how to preserve it, and most importantly how and when to use it. Today Little Hawk was visiting his family and enjoying playing hoops and skipping rocks on the water.

This was the busy season. It was food gathering time: hak' wa7, roots, shoots, greens, mushrooms, and freshly caught Spring Salmon. Cedar roots were harvested along with cedar bark. Cedar trees were cut to make canoes of varying sizes and uses. Various grasses were harvested to be used in cedar root basketry making during the winter months. The hunters brought fresh meat to the village and shared it with elders and Ol' Griz. It was the custom. The village looked after him in return for his service to the people. Little Hawk and the other children took part in these activities. Everyone participated in the well-being of the village and did their part according to their abilities.

Little Hawk was eleven years old now. He had grown 6 inches this past summer. He was growing tall and quite strong from his many activities. His teachers were pleased with his progress. From his warrior uncle he was now a skilled tracker, in all seasons of the year. He would need this skill in a few years when he left on his four year journey. He was good with tools and could make necessary tools for survival. The plant world was second nature to him now as well. His natural ability to absorb information in the dreamtime was almost complete.

He and Great Papa had some interesting adventures in the dreamtime. They had met many Ancient Ones and Spirits of the Ancestors and sat with them in Circle. They had witnessed the passing over of many souls of the people who had rejoiced to be reunited with loved ones, especially with parents and other favorite relatives. There were sad occasions as well, the unexpected or accidental passing over of someone in the community, especially a newborn or young child. Great Papa assured Little Hawk that when this occurred that the sacred spirit of the young one merely had to touch mother earth for a short time, and then return to the spirit world.

It was a busy time of the year. The annual gathering of the people was behind them, preparations for the hunting season were underway. Little Hawk was excited to be taking part in his first hunt this year.

He eagerly got ready every day. First thing in the dawn, he went for his swim, then ran for five miles, had a bowl of warm food and began his chores for the day. His uncle, who was his hunting and tracking teacher as well, showed him how to clean and care for his gun. His father had given him a pony and the boy and the horse bonded easily. Little Hawk took good care of his horse which he named Lightning. Lightning seemed to have a sixth sense as well and the two of them spent many happy hours together.

The hunting base camp was across the river this year. Canoes and make-shift rafts were unloaded and the camp took shape in a matter of a few hours. Drying and stretching racks were repaired, wood gathered and cooking fires were lit. The people were fed and settled down for the night. Ol' Griz sat by the fire waiting for the dreamtime. He travelled to the stars and returned to his sleeping place.
"Ah, I see you," he said to the Elk and the Mountain Goat nation. The four legged acknowledged the old wise man. They had moved down to the lush meadows to feed on the rich wild hay in preparation for the harsh winter months ahead. At dawn the next morning Ol' Griz told the people that he had dreamed and that the animals had shown themselves.

This year his uncle, who was his teacher, would be hunting deer with his nephew. Little Hawk was very honoured. His uncle was also the Bear Hunter for the community. He had assigned an experienced hunter to go with his usual bear hunting partner this year. Little hawk recalled the story of First Deer and First Hunter. He resolved to honour his first hunt in the time honoured manner of his community.

They set out on horseback at dawn to a place that deer were fond of making their nests. They rode confidently taking in the terrain and being watchful for potential windfalls and snags on the trees around them. They rode for several miles. They came to a clearing which had a stream running through it. The riders dismounted and with guns in hand, walked quietly, watching carefully for any movement. The mist was clearing. Little Hawk saw the four point deer ahead of him at the stream. Little Hawk got ready. He said a silent prayer to the spirit of the deer and took careful aim as the deer turned his magnificent head. The boy took his shot and the deer went down.

Little Hawk experienced many emotions in mere seconds. Thoughts spun through his mind. He was thankful that he had said his prayer thoughts before shooting the deer. He was proud to be taking his place as a hunter for his family. He was thankful to have his uncle witness his success. He was proud to be able to give his mother the hide to make a shirt or moccasins with. He and his uncle worked together in comfortable silence to clean and skin the animal. They rode back to base camp, happy in the knowledge that Smitty had heard the single shot and would have food ready for their return.

Great Papa and Smitty were in camp and came forward to congratulate Little Hawk on his successful first hunt.
"Did you eat a bit of the heart?" asked Great Papa.
"Yes," Little Hawk replied.
"Good," the old man nodded.

He gave the heart and liver to Smitty to prepare. Smitty heated his cooking pans and added fresh wild onions to the pan of sizzling meat. It was shared ceremonially with the community and the rest of the meat was distributed to the elders. It was the custom. Little Hawk's mother had the cleaning and stretching rack ready and she smiled as she began the process of making the hide ready for future use.

The hunting camp activities were almost done. The berries and greens were drying. The racks were full of wind dried salmon. The community had worked hard all year to prepare for the harsh unrelenting winter months. Wood had been gathered and was still an activity that each person took time for each day. Memories of other winters past without these necessities kept the people busy in preparation. Life returned to its normal routine after the hunting season.

Ol' Griz knew that it was time to prepare his great grandson's family for Little Hawk's four day Fast. He gathered the family and talked to them about the ceremony. It was decided that Little Hawk would follow the protocol that was set down for an aspiring medicine man. Little Hawk would do his Fast before the first snows of the year came. Ceremony was conducted every day in the sweat house.

His family had prepared his place on the mountain where he was to be tested. Little Hawk would not have food or water during the four days and nights of his time on the mountain. He would be all alone as well. Little Hawk needed to draw on his past experience of his two days and nights on the mountain. He believed that he was ready. His Uncle and his Father accompanied him to his place. They helped prepare Little Hawk's sleeping place with boughs and created his sacred space. They painted him with red ochre. He was given a stone bowl carved into the form of a bear and smudge. They silently left him.

It was a sunny day. Little Hawk looked at his surroundings. This was a new site for him, further from the village. It was a good place with a clear view all round. He enjoyed the feel of the sunshine and the warmth. As soon as the sun went down the air became chilled. He reached for his outer clothing and his blanket and settled himself on the boughs and began his prayers and songs while the smudge was lit.

The night closed in and Little Hawk had a restful night. At dawn he was awakened by the absence of the sounds of birds and animals. He looked up and saw the Morning Star, he offered his morning prayers. He felt the reverence that the birds and animals exhibited at this time of morning. His heart soared. He was in awe of the creation around himself. He began to sing his gratitude, the animals and birds joined in. Little Hawk understood something was changing within himself. He became still and the peacefulness soaked into his being, and so it went through the day.

The second night again was uneventful with only phantoms clouding his dreams. The next day Little Hawk felt lonely and he prayed and sang the songs his family had taught him until the feeling passed. The third day and night were harder. Little hawk drew on the information that his teachers had given him. He prayed and sang until he fell asleep again. During the fourth night he left his sleeping place when his Spirit Guide came. They visited many realms during this time. Dawn came and Little Hawk awoke. His Uncle and his Father gathered up the boughs into a bundle to bring to the fire and they walked back to the village and to the sweat house behind the cabin.

Great Papa/Ol' Griz was very pleased with Little Hawk. During the feast to celebrate his first successful four day Fast, Ol' Griz had a new name ready to give Little Hawk.
"From this day forward," Ol' Griz began, "you shall be called, Bear Claw."
Bear Claw beamed his happiness and expressed his love and gratitude to his family and community. Bear Claw's next Fast would take place in the spring and the one after that would take place at the Summer Solstice.

The time was drawing near. Ol' Griz felt it in his bones. He was feeling his age in small uncomfortable ways, a little stiffening of the knees an aching back after chopping wood or getting water. He enjoyed walking and doing his ceremonies. Time seemed to be speeding up or so it seemed to him at times.

Bear Claw was now nearing his 15th year. He had grown quite tall, six feet already, and was strong from his activities. He was a favorite with his community because of his willingness to help anyone who needed help. He gathered his friends around him and together they made winter wood for the elders, went out food fishing and hunting for them. He still lived in the cabin with Great Papa and Smitty by choice and with his family's blessing. Bear Claw enjoyed the love and trust that he had earned. He did not make his special teachings an obstacle between himself and his friends nor did he let it interfere with his outgoing nature.

Ol' Griz sent a runner to call his family together. It was time to begin the preparations for Bear Claw's fourth Fast. It would take place on the Winter Solstice. This was the time of year when the final preparations for the coming winter months was done. The family members gathered to listen to Great Papa's words and the plans made for this event.

"As you all know," Ol' Griz began, "Bear Claw has been my apprentice for many years, since just before his sixth year. He has fulfilled his tasks well. He has learned the spiritual language of journeying to the other realms. He knows the sign posts that guide him safely back. He has learned the survival skills and much more from his relatives. He has shown himself to be fearless. I believe that he is ready to complete the fourth and final Fast of his initiation." Ol' Griz invited discussion and comment and they were in agreement that it was now time for Bear Claw to complete his initiation before going out into the world for four years to find his special gifts as a Healer/Medicine Man.

He would sit in a hole in the ground that was dug down six feet by four feet. He would have his bear robe for warmth and comfort. The hole would be covered so that there was no light allowed. Bear Claw prepared as he had done before. Four days of ceremony in the sweat house; during this time he purged himself with cascara bark tea. His mother prepared a nourishing meal for her beloved son before undertaking his Fast.

Respected adult men went to the site of the planned fasting place to prepare the ground for this most difficult test. Ol' Griz made the arduous journey to supervise the work. Prayers and ceremony were said during every stage of the preparations. Bear Claw's best friend was chosen to be lowered into the hole and place the cedar and fir boughs at the bottom of the fasting place. He prayed very hard for his friend and vowed that he would always be there for Bear Claw. He felt in awe of Bear Claw's life choice and his dedication to fulfilling his vision. Everything was ready and the men made their way back down the mountain.

Bear Claw was waiting. Ol' Griz painted his great grandson with red ochre and placed a red bandana on his head. He dressed and nodded that he was ready. His Uncle and his father accompanied him up to the mountain. Once again his Uncle had the stone bear carved bowl with smudge. He smudged his nephew. Bear Claw manoeuvred himself to the edge of the hole and dropped down with is bear hide blanket.

He arranged the bear hide around him and indicated that he was ready to have the covering placed over the hole. His relatives worked diligently to make sure that the covering was fully placed so that all light was blocked. They silently and reverently walked down the mountain.

The village was hushed as were the animals. The people of the village went about their business quietly. Children were mainly kept indoors. No one was out of doors after dusk. There was a definite chill in the air after the sun went down. Bear Claw's relatives took turns doing ceremony in the sweat house and keeping vigil day and night. Food was offered and burned for him every day. Bear Claw prayed and sang until he fell asleep. His Spirit Guide came and they took journeys to many places that Bear Claw would journey to in the near future. Bear Claw journeyed during most of the time. On the fourth night he was given instructions from his Spirit Guide that would astonish everyone in the village by the next morning.

Bear Claw's relatives finished their ceremonies in the sweat house after midnight and went home to rest. His Uncle, Father, Ol' Griz and Smitty sat around keeping the sacred fire going through the remainder of the night. Shortly after the first rays of sunlight appeared, the men made their journey to the mountain to bring

Bear Claw down. They came singing a greeting and to rouse Bear Claw. The men began removing the covers from the hole where Bear Claw was sitting. It is hard to describe the men's collective shock to peer down the hole and to find there was no one there, just the bear robe.

Ol' Griz was sitting alone by the sacred fire at his sweat house when he heard a 'whooshing sound'. He thought for a moment and remembered that sound. It was the sound of a Spirit Being flashing by. Ol' Griz stood up and looked in the direction where the sound had come from. It had come from the sweat house. He cautiously approached the covering of the doorway. He carefully drew back the covering and allowed a bit of light into the dark. There sat Bear Claw, still in a trance.

Ol' Griz closed the opening. He went and sat down on a log to wait for the men to return from the mountain. They returned shortly after. They shared mixed feelings on what to say to Ol' Griz about his missing great grandson. Ol' Griz took pity on them and indicated that Bear Claw was in the sweat house. Ol' Griz took charge of the situation by indicating that they were to get ready with drums and get comfortable as they were going to sing and drum quietly so that Bear Claw would return to himself fully in mind body and spirit. The men sang many songs to restore their relative wholly and fully to them.

Bear Claw awoke and scratched on the covering of the sweat house. His relatives looked to Ol' Griz for direction. He indicated that they were to open the covering slowly to allow Bear Claw's eyes time to adjust to the daylight, the bandana was drawn down to cover his eyes. Ol' Griz stared at his apprentice and raised both of his hands up to indicate his great respect for Bear Claw's astonishing feat. Ol' Griz and the men joined Bear Claw in the sweat house to complete the ceremony. Bear Claw told them of his experiences on the mountain and the things he had been shown. He finished by telling them that he would undertake his four year journey away from his people in the early spring. None of the people present that day would ever forget the ceremony, it would be talked about around village fires for years.

The women had been preparing a feast for Bear Claw's return. There was much excitement as they all knew that what had happened was a rare occurrence.

Blessings and prayers and songs were sung. Ol' Griz stood up to make an announcement, the crowd hushed as they did when their leader got ready to speak. "Bear Claw, you shall be known by a different name from today forward," he said. "The name you have earned is Nkasusa, it means: 'Moves Like A Ghost'." There was silence for a moment, and the crowd spontaneously cheered this choice.

The first snowfall began. There was something hanging over the little cabin by the edge of the village. There was a sense of time passing too quickly and an urgency to speak of many things before time ran out. Nkasusa thought about this and came to the realization that in a few months he would begin his journey of four years. He understood that Great Papa was concerned that he had missed teaching Nkasusa an important lesson to insure his survival beyond the borders of their territory.

In an effort to distract his beloved Papa, Nkasusa asked him to tell his story of how he had become to be known by the name Ol' Griz. Traders from faraway lands knew of him by his reputation as a fair minded negotiator. By others he was known to be a great healer and by still others he was known to be a great leader. His Papa was guided by the principles of his predecessors. He took care of the people's needs. He was fair minded in a dispute situation, listening carefully, evaluating the information and reaching a fair assessment before speaking. He was stern when he needed to be, Great Papa was also kind, loving, generous and a man of courage.

Great Papa scratched his head of greying hair before beginning to tell his story. Smitty was present.
"Nkasusa", he began, "I have tried to bring you up in the same way that our relatives brought me up. I had the same teachings as you have been taught. However," and Great Papa smiled as he continued, "you have exceeded my experience when I was the same age as you are now."
"In what way Great Papa?" he asked.
"You've Shape Shifted at a much earlier age than I did. I did not learn to do this until I was on my four year journey." They all smiled. That is as it needs to be; the younger generation exceeds the efforts of the older generations. Nkasusa relaxed when he heard this.

"You understand that it will take four years to complete your training to be a good medicine man?" he asked.
"Yes, I do."
"You will be tested in many ways. Shape Shifting will be useful to you when you are in a difficult situation. Do you understand this?"
"Yes, I do Great Papa."
"It will be tempting to use this skill for your own purpose, but you must not do so, it is important that we use our spiritual gifts wisely and for the good of others."
Again, the answer was "Yes, Great Papa."
"When I had completed my four year journey it was difficult to return to the people, not because I did not love my family, but because I had not spoken to another human being during my absence. Also, there is a stench in the air of people living in a village. It is not noticeable to others, but when you have been living in the bush there is no build up of refuse."
"Oh," said Nkasusa in surprise. He thought about this information and realized that great Papa was preparing him for the future and that perhaps Great Papa would not be here for his return from his travels.
Great Papa continued: "When I completed my four years and returned to the village, I kept to the edges of the village for many days. I was waiting for someone to

notice my presence. Finally my father saw me and recognized me. You see, I had grown several inches since we last saw each other. I was kind of wild you see. He was not afraid to approach me; instead he said that he was expecting my return during this season of the year. We went to the sweat house and did ceremony together. He allowed me the time to return fully to myself. We finished our ceremony and went to the istken where we had a simple but nourishing meal together. Father knew that I needed quiet and privacy for awhile, so he left me there. He brought food that mother had prepared and we would talk for awhile. Then Mother came to see me, it was too much for her, I had grown taller and was now a man. Her strong emotion broke down my shyness to be around people again. I embraced my mother in gratitude to be in her presence once again."
"Mother seems to take charge of my life," he laughed.
"Your chosen one has waited for your return. Would you like to have a visit with her? We will be present as that is the custom," my Mother said.
"Kika'kiam looked forward to this meeting. Nkasusa had plenty of work ahead of him to make a proper home for his future wife. They had plenty of help and soon an addition was made onto the existing longhouse. They had the rest of the summer to collect the necessary food for the long winter months ahead. The annual gathering took place and we were joined in a marriage alliance that was very happy," he said.
"Several years went by and your grandfather was born. We continued to follow the seasons, finding enjoyment with our lives and our community. Then I began having dreams again. I found myself with my Spirit Guide more and more often. We would journey in the dreamtime. One night it occurred to me to ask him if there was a purpose to his visits. He indicated that there was."
"What is it?" I asked.
"We in the spirit world have been watching over you since your successful return from your journey. We believe that it is time for you to take your final test."
"What is that?"
"It is time for you to go out to kill a grizzly bear, leaving your obsidian knife in his jaws during his last charge toward you."
"For the first time that I could remember, my heart gave a nudge and I felt a momentary twinge of fear. It passed quickly as I realized that there was a greater purpose to be served in their request. The purpose was to prepare me to become 'Chief of Chiefs'. I would become the leader of all of the tribes within our Territory. It was a position of great respect beyond our borders."
"I said farewell to my family, Keek-lok-ik was pregnant once again. We did ceremony for several days to prepare for this step in my life. I left the comfort of home and packed my rifle and other gear and headed out. There was a mountain range to the west of me, many miles trekking and two day journey to the base of the mountain. It was the base of our holy mountain, Nsvq'ts (In'shuch'ck). I knew these mountains well and made a small camp with a lean-to and made a fire. Tomorrow I would begin to climb this formidable mountain. It was said that a person had to be spiritually prepared to undertake this journey."

"Early the next morning it was chilly and I made a fire and heated the tea that I had brought with me. I offered up prayers, ate sparingly and began walking. It was steep and rough country with glacier fed creeks. When the sun was at its' highest point I came across a highland lake. I stripped and jumped in, it was very cold and I stifled a holler. I did not wish to give our four legged too much advance notice of my coming he laughed. I got out of the water and dressed quickly and proceeded to the three quarter mark on the mountain. I had been taught that everything growing above that was not to be disturbed. It was late afternoon by now, so I made camp once again. This time I did not make a camp fire."

"At dawn the next morning I splashed my face with water and had a drink and filled my canteen. In the dreamtime I was given an indication of where to find the grizzly bear so I headed out in that direction. Around mid morning, I began to feel the hairs prickle at the back of my neck and I could smell that the bear was in the vicinity. Sure enough, there he was in a clearing, eating berries. I looked over the situation. I was behind an old stump. The grizzly bear became aware of my presence as well, as he had a very sensitive nose to smell anything unusual in his territory. And on that day, the unusual smell was me, a human being."

"I believe that we both understood our role that day. The grizzly bear was mature and had no reason to fear the smell of human beings as yet or their weapons. A gun was not common in those days. The huge grizzly bear stood up on his hind legs and looked in my direction and he became agitated. He gave a loud warning growl. I stood up, the bear got down on all four legs and made further warning growls. I stood my ground. The bear charged, I fired, he was very close to me and I could feel his hot breath, I had made a good shot and that slowed down his charge noticeably, and just as he took a faltering step, his mouth was open and I pushed the seven inch obsidian spear with points on both ends into his jaws. Our eyes met, and with his last breaths his power flowed into me. I wept, for both of us, and then I gave thanks, for the Grizzly Bear Spirit that was now mine. I turned our relative's head toward the west and sang a song. I rested for a short while and then began the process of hanging the bear and dressing him out according to tradition. I left his huge carcass for other predators, it is also the custom. Our people did not eat bear meat."

"The reason the bear robe that you wore in your Fourth Year Fast fit you so well is that it was the grizzly bear hide from the hunt on that day."
Nkasusa gulped and all of a sudden felt very humble indeed. Great Papa and Smitty smiled because they knew that this young man was a humble man.

Great Papa continued: "A feast was held upon my return with the head and hide of the huge grizzly bear. My family took it and prepared a stretching and drying rack. The hide was treated and made into a robe. The name Ol' Griz had nothing do to with my age but the people wished to honour me and it was a name of endearment as much as anything."

"What is it?" asked Ol' Griz, "Your eyes are as big as an owl's."
Nkasusa recovered as best he could. "Will I do that too?" he asked.
Ol' Griz looked at him and replied: "Only if you have a vision that shows you that you need to do this." His apprentice relaxed once again.

The Watchmen who were in the high mountain look out places sent their apprentice Watchmen as runners to inform Ol' Griz and the community that winter would come early this year. The early signs were that the beavers were building their winter houses early, and the birds were getting ready to fly south. The annual gathering was cut short and every able bodied person increased their efforts to gather food and enough fish to last them through a hard winter. Nkasusa and his companions increased their work load to help provide the elders with enough wood and kindling for the winter fires. It was a severe winter, which started with a cold snap which came suddenly and lasted for many days. The wind howled and the snow fell. And so it went for four moon cycles. False Spring came with a Chinook wind, and the people came out of their houses, rejoicing, then it was several weeks before the sun shone with any warmth.

With the coming of spring, Ol' Griz knew that it was time for Nkasusa to begin his four year journey. They had many discussions about the items that he could bring with him in his pack sack. He would need dried tea leaves and tobacco. He would also need a means to start his camp fires. They decided that the white man's matches were acceptable, only if they were kept dry; he also carried a flint with him. He packed his wool blanket and a change of sturdy moccasins that his mother had made. He brought the rifle and some ammunition. He would occasionally need to kill a moose or other large animal for winter food, and prepare the hide for clothing or moccasins. He also packed dried meat and ts'wan and small metal cans that the white man had discarded to heat water and cook food in. His father gave him a big knife with a bear carved into the handle. He carried a skinning knife as well and an axe head. He knew how to make the other tools he would need.

It was a sunny morning when Nkasusa left the village. There had been ceremonies beforehand. A feast was prepared with precious stores of food that had been carefully kept for this special event. All of the community turned out for this feast. The social dancing began and everyone had a good time, they raised their hands up in farewell to Nkasusa; no one said good bye because we had no words for good bye in our language.

As agreed with his Great Papa, Nkasusa walked out from the village in the direction of north toward Stega;yn (Stein Valley). There were potential pit falls here he was told and he needed to pay particular attention to protocols to the unseen presence of the Spirit Guardians of this sacred place. To avoid angering the mighty serpents who guarded the gateway he must stop at the Y on the trail.

When the mighty serpent appeared —and he would as he was one of the guardians — Nkasusa must be ready. He was to remain calm and put his pack sack on the ground in front of himself with his rifle on top of everything else. He must have a tobacco offering ready. Nkasusa followed the protocol but was unprepared for the height of the guardian serpent, whose head was about three feet above his head. The guardian spirit did not smell very good either. He knew that there were two serpent guardians at this point and also knew that he was on the correct pathway as it was the serpent on the right side which had shown itself.

Nkasusa stood perfectly still and the large serpent bent down from his towering height and sniffed the contents of the pack sack and the rifle. Nkasusa quickly projected what he needed the rifle for. The Guardian Serpent moved back to his place and the young man left his gift of tobacco on that spot.

Nkasusa silently gave thanks to his teachers and to Great Papa for preparing him for the times of meeting with the guardian spirits in these faraway lands. It was several days walk to get here. He continued onward, watching the rock formations and reading the pictographs left on them. They were his markers. When it became deep dusk, he stopped and made a lean-to camp. He made a small fire and made tea. He ate and rested. He continued northward for another day and then he suddenly noticed that the trees and underbrush that he was used to, were thinning out and that the air was drier as well.

From now on, he realized, he must stay on the hundreds of years old bear trails, instead of the trails left by the strangers who now inhabited this homeland. He must at all costs stay away from human beings.

He steadily pushed northward, finding fresh greens and shoots along the way and pine mushrooms that were a treat, wild asparagus in the swampy areas were greatly enjoyed. He journeyed on throughout the spring and the landscape changed subtly, but now there were stubby pine trees and large animals like moose and elk which told him that it was soon time to find a place to live through the coming winter months. He stayed by a lake for several weeks setting snares for the wild birds who were coming in. He used his snare to catch rabbits and grouse, most of which he dried for winter use. Goose and duck grease would keep him healthy throughout the winter. He gathered wild tea leaves as well. He had time to dry the elk meat and put it away in a cache. He made a coat and boots from the hide. He was kept busy every day. It became a habit to gather wood every day, on his walks back to his camp.

He went to the river and found that he could catch salmon with the dip netting that he attached to a long pole. He made a rack and dried his catch in the sun and wind. He built an istken in the ground. Winter came quickly and it was very cold, snow piled up. He heard wolves and coyotes howling in the distance. He conserved his energy when the wind howled and the trees cracked and broke in the extreme cold. During breaks in the weather he climbed the ladder and went out to gather wood falls and get water.

One day Nkasusa noticed a change in the weather. It was still cold with lots of snow on the ground. There was a definite change coming. He must begin to prepare to move on to the next part of his journey. He heard them high overhead, the geese were returning to the area. He rejoiced in this knowledge and began to get his snares ready. These birds were big and wary and had big beaks and snapped at anything. He observed them for several days. He was hungry for fresh meat and looked for fresh greens in his daily walks. After several attempts, he learned that it was easier to snare them in the semi darkness of the morning. He built a fire, singed the feathers and cooked the geese on the open fire. He felt rather than saw the eyes upon him, so he took the left over flesh and bones and walked a good distance from his camp and left them.

It was time to move on. The rough grass was coming up and the trees were starting to bud. He got his pack sack ready and took apart the axe handle, leaving it behind as well as the fishing pole. He did take the dried fish and meat with him. He knew that he needed to continue on northward for a time and so he did. It was uncharted territory and he didn't meet any people, although he had seen signs and passed over cold trails. He continued on for a moon cycle, steadily north and slightly east.

One day he was intrigued by a mountain south and east of where he was and decided that this was the sign that he had been waiting for. The mountain shone pink in the distance and became a beacon for him. Nkasusa was comfortable with this decision. The landscape was easier to travel through compared to his homeland, which was a primal rain forest with lots of underbrush.

One sunny spring day as he walked along, he heard the earth rumbling and looked in the direction of the noise. He was astonished to see his first live buffalo herd. He knew that he was definitely in a new territory. He also knew that these people's relatives in the south of this territory liked to come to his homeland and ambush the women and children and kidnap them to make slaves of them.

He was aware of this, but today he watched the herd of buffalo race over the valley with total absorption. He gave thanks for his first sight of these magnificent animals. He watched with fascination while the herd raced on heedless of the terrain. A large section of the animals turned and surged across the grass land while a good number of them raced toward a cliff that was hidden by a tangle of brush and fallen trees. They went plummeting to their death over the high cliff wall. Then he saw the people from this homeland racing along behind the herd on horseback. They and their horses were painted and the hunters were screaming and encouraging their horses onward. Then, when they saw the herd veer off, they changed direction abruptly and slowed their mounts to a walk. The horses were excited and pranced around until they were reined in by the rider. He watched and saw other people at the bottom of the steep gorge. They moved in quickly and began to cut the throats of the buffalo that had fallen into the trap. They left distinctive shafts in the animals that they were claiming as theirs.

Nkasusa instinctively offered up prayers for the spirits of the slain buffalo. He left a tobacco offering at the spot that he had witnessed the hunt. He went on his way, veering north again. He kept walking until dark, made camp and rolled up in his robe and fell asleep quickly. During the night he had visitors. These visitors came to him in the dreamtime. They were the relatives of the buffalo who had veered off avoiding the trap set by the strangers of this homeland.

Nkasusa was familiar with the story of the First Deer and wondered if these buffalo had the same understanding of helping their two legged relatives. He felt the warm breath and wool tickling his face. He stayed still but opened his eyes. In front of him was a large animal's head. That was all that he could see. The animal snuffled a welcome and licked Nkasusa's face. He felt the rough tongue and chuckled to himself. He became aware of the buffalo's eyes and felt the reason that his relatives taught him that we are all related. They gazed at one another for a time, and then the buffalo conveyed a message to him.
"When you have reached the furthest part of your journey and begin to return to your homeland, return to the place where you made your tobacco offering. Buffalo Nation will help you with your quest."
He went north for a day or so then decided that it was time to go south and east again.

Now he observed there were lots of scrub trees and large swamp areas. Moose and black bears seemed to make their home here. He saw plenty of chokecherry bushes and a good smelling plant. It was new to him, but he trusted his instincts and picked some and made tea with it. It was very good. He picked more to carry with him. Ah, his memory of this tea returned to him and he remembered that it was available in the high swampy part of a lake north of his home territory.

He continued travelling along the ridges headed east. It was time to find a place to spend the winter. He was still in the high country and knew that it was going to be another cold hard winter. He stayed at this altitude because he had seen the remnants of animal trapping along the way. He got down to work, he worked tirelessly every day. He made another istken somewhat smaller because of the size of the trees. It would be sufficient. He filled the space between the rafters with wood for his small cooking and heating needs. He once again shot a moose for his winter meat supply and dried it and made pemmican with chokecherries for nourishment. He had kept his supply of dried salmon dry and that was a comfort to him.

It was colder than anything he had ever experienced before. It was a long cold winter with very little if any sunlight. He knew that he was still far to the north. He was very grateful for his teachings and had dreams of home and his family. He felt that Great Papa was doing well. In fact, Ol' Griz was slowly getting weaker. Winter was the hardest on his health. He prayed daily for the well being of his family. He had cause to offer up prayers for himself a few times during the winter and was glad of the relative safety of his istken house. A wolf pack had a den on a nearby hillside.

Several times they had come in the darkness to howl near the opening of his underground house. At such times he made a bigger fire and some heat must have escaped and the pack settled down on his roof. At daybreak they were always gone.

Spring came with the usual signs of birds flying north and snow melting everywhere. He got ready to begin his journey again. He put his tools and cache of food in his pack sack along with his blanket. He began walking south bearing east. He came to a large body of water; it was too large to see the other side. His curiosity overcame him and he cupped his hands in the water, drew out some water and tasted it. It was fresh water. The water was a very large lake. He laughed. He started to follow the contours of the shoreline southward. After a day of walking he saw a camp that had been left for some time. It was trapping country, he reasoned. There was a broken birch bark canoe left abandoned. He must be very careful not to walk into a village, or walk too close to the trappers drop off place. By now he could smell human beings from a great distance and found it to be more than he could cope with.

He continued his walk southward and he realized that he was at the curve of the big lake. He walked around the lake and went north and east again. He continued his journey and saw that the people of this homeland lived in longhouses made of different materials, but longhouses never the less. He was intrigued by this commonality with his homeland. The houses were made of birch bark. They were deserted at this time of year, and he supposed for the same reasons that his longhouses were closed at this time of year. He reasoned that the owners would return in the autumn.

Nkasusa decided that this was a good place to settle down for winter. He was beside another large lake. He did his usual preparations and made a birch bark house for himself. He lined it with the moose hides that he had made. The meat was dried and he got wood which he hoped would be enough for his needs. Autumn was very colourful here. The first snow fell in December and fell for long periods of time. The sun would shine and there was the odd warm day. Then snow would fall again keeping Nkasusa indoors for half a moon. He solemnly promised himself that he would make the best of things. He would not return to this country again. It turned out to be a soggy muddy spring. He noticed notches on some maple trees and sap was running out and dripping onto the ground. This was something new and interesting. He tasted the sap and it was sweet. He hung around the area to see who would come by and what they would do with the sweet tasting sap. After a few days of waiting, he saw some u'wa'mitcw coming toward the trees and they had rough looking buckets with them. They tapped a plug into the tree and set the bucket under the plug. The sap ran faster into the bucket and they emptied the bucket several times. When they were satisfied that they had gotten all the sap they needed, they pulled the plug and left with their bounty of the sweet sap. "This must be their first harvest of the spring," he thought to himself.
These people were clever. He also thought that it must be good medicine.

He used one of his metal pots to gather sap and enjoyed it sparingly for many days. He felt rejuvenated by this new medicine. He enjoyed the sunshine during the day and noticed that it was still cold at night. "It is time to move on," he thought. He gathered his tools and food and all of his belongings into his pack sack and started walking southward. He had seen enough of the lakes and swamps and the mosquitoes of this part of the country.

Nkasusa walked southward for the remainder of the spring. It was interesting country; he saw more of the buffalo and antelopes and big jack rabbits for the first time. He stayed away from the villages and from the barking dogs that lived there. It was very flat country with long grasses and very little else. He saw the places where entire villages had camped for hunting. He walked over burnt areas caused by lightning.

Half way through the early summer he changed direction and started to walk north and west. He longed to see trees again. More than that, he longed to be in the mountains. He was walking with purpose now. He needed to return to the place where he had travelled in the first year of his journey. It was summer when he found his old camp, which was close to the buffalo jump off place. He rebuilt his living quarters and prepared for winter once again.

Snow began falling and Nkasusa was snug in his istken with a small fire and hot food and tea. He got into his bedroll after saying his prayers for his family and community. He closed his eyes and drifted off into a light sleep. Sometime during the night his visitors, the Buffalo Spirits, returned to visit him.
"We have been watching your progress," the spirits indicated, because they communicated by a form of telepathy and visions. "You will receive the gift of changing events and preventing events from happening", they said.
He accepted this knowledge and these new skills that would make him the best healer in his nation.

Several moons passed. He was glad that this was his last winter away from his family. One night he had a vision of his beloved Great Papa, he felt him, as if he was very close by.
"I have come to let you know that I am ready to pass into the spirit world," he said.
"No," Nkasusa said, "I have received the gift of changing events and I can save you from leaving." Great Papa said that he was aware of this, and said: "Do not attempt to touch me, Nkasusa, or you will lose your way and you will not find your way home to the family and community who are expecting you in the spring."
"I know that you are right, Great Papa. You taught me to respect the life cycles of all things and now I must respect the close of your life cycle." He offered tobacco to the fire and calmed himself. He felt his beloved Papa's spirit whoosh out of the istken. The next morning he started to make himself snowshoes. He would start travelling home and checked his supply of dried food.
"I have enough to last while I travel home," he thought.

And so it was that he arrived home, pulling a make shift sled with the carcass of a moose that he had killed the day before.
Smitty was the first person to see him. He thought to himself: "I did hear a rifle shot across the mountain tops yesterday, and so who else could it be but Nkasusa." Smitty, who had witnessed his relative Ol' Griz return to the village another age ago, knew that it would take some time for Nkasusa to feel comfortable among humans.

Smitty walked backward to the istken that was clean and ready to be occupied. Nkasusa followed him and entered the comfort of home. His mother cooked food and delivered it to the istken every day. He overcame his shyness and reached out to his mother and sister, then to his father and they became a strong family once again.

It seemed like no time at all before the village became the place to come to seek healing and advice from Nkasusa. The community built him a house and brought everything that he and his wife would need to begin their life journey together. The time would come, many decades in the future when Nkasusa would receive his final name of distinction, for the moment his life was full and he was content.

∫